FROM THE GROUND TO THE BIRDSONG

flipped eye publishing
London

From the Ground to the Birdsong
Barbican Young Poets 2024

First published by flipped eye publishing © 2024
Copyright © 2024, Barbican Centre
Cover Design © 2024 flipped eye publishing
Author Images © 2024, Ray Roberts

All Rights Reserved. The rights of the individual authors to be identified as contributors to this anthology have been asserted in accordance with Section 77 of the Copyright, Designs and Patents Act 1988.

No part of this publication may be reproduced, stored in a retrieval system, or transmitted, in any form or by any means, electronic, mechanical, photocopying, recording, or otherwise, without the written permission of the appropriate individual author, nor may it be otherwise circulated in any form of binding or cover other than that in which it is published and without a similar condition including this condition being imposed on the subsequent purchaser.

This book is typeset in Trajan Pro and Palatino Linotype.

flipped eye publishing
www.flippedeye.net

ISBN-13: 978-1-905233-89-2

From the Ground to the Birdsong

Barbican Young Poets
2024

barbican

From the Ground to the Birdsong
Barbican Young Poets 2024

FOREWORD	7
Shyamli B	
if revolution was a wall	9
Nomakhwezi Becker	
A city, dreaming	11
Summoned (The Wake)	13
Zad El Bacha	
An Arab killed in Palestine	16
Geraint Ellis	
G.F.A.R.	17
Lava	19
Nathalia Samhil Gonzalez Gutierrez	
Habeas Corpus	20
oxytocin clumps at the cable input entrance (2019)	21
Marianne Habeshaw	
First time eating emu burgers at the bird sanctuary	22
How to: Modern Therapy	24
Oli Isaac	
vultures will only care about me when i'm dead, or dying, or sick	25
why can't i say it straight?	27
Noah Jacob	
if the black holes come for us	29
salmon run	31
Kerrica Kendall	
Morsel in a history	36
Palatable	39
Rachel Lewis	
Honestly	41
Diamond paradelle	42
Bluey Little	
Archimedes' Principle	43
when their bones are picked, may a flower no more	44

Katie O'Pray
    In my slice of city   45
    Becoming Auntie   46
Beth Phillips
    pit bonk wench   47
    when my mother became an egg   48
Jess Rahman-González
    I told u hell is emotional intimacy & u still kissed me
    (a cento)   49
Amani Saeed
    In flagrante   50
    When I come back   51
Lucas Sheridan
    Plucked   53
Maeve Slattery
    Massage   54
    In a Moment of Future Brightness   55
Ishita Uppadhayay
    English Education   57
    Machine   58
Vera K Yuen
    Self-Portrait as Lampshade   59
Biographies

FOREWORD

Every long-lived experience is made up of a series of discrete moments. Steps along the path from wherever the history began to wherever we've arrived at, now.

We have approximately 16 years worth of history to celebrate at this point in the BYP programme, depending on how you count. 16 years of poets, poems, prompts, workshop nights in the Frobisher rooms, guest tutors, assistant tutors, producers, showcases and anthologies. 16 years of experimentation. 16 years of collaboratively creating a safe space for poets to try, fail, fail again, and continue learning from those failures. 16 years of framing the notion that failure is something we need not fear. 16 years of bringing different voices and poetics together to spark off each other, to push each other in new directions, to celebrate together whatever it is that happens when we put pen to paper or fingers on keys attempting to record a sequence of words that somehow captures whatever vision we've been struck by, even as that vision unfolds itself before us. 16 years of celebrating process over (but not to the exclusion of) product. 16 years of nurturing a practice-based developmental programme. 16 years of cultivating a sense of love, attention and care for the work, the people, the space and all the other essential parts that constitute the kind of programme BYP is, has been and should continue to be as the years roll on.

Each cohort for the last 16 years has had its own character, texture and concerns. Look back through any of the forewords I've written for these anthologies, and you'll note how heavily I lean on the notion of community (it wouldn't be a BYP anthology foreword if I didn't squeeze the word in a handful of times). This year, more than ever before, it feels like the sense of community this cohort constitutes has emerged as an active, empowered construct. And with all my various hats on (facilitator, programme director, poet) I'm moved by what that means and represents. At its best, this programme isn't just about "nurturing talent" or "gateways to creative industries" or any of the other corporate lingua sometimes used to frame, justify, promote or rationalise work like this. This is work that explores what it means to live (creatively and professionally) with heart and mind open. This is work that explores what it means to be human in an all-too-often dehumanising world. This is work that protests, decries, declaims and sings.

Yes, those last sentences blur the lines between my musings about the programme and comments on the work contained within this anthology. And yes, that's intentional. I have little interest in abstracting the work on these pages from the experience each of these poets went through during their time this year. And I don't have the words or enough room here to detail that experience—that could be the basis of a separate publication in itself. But if you weren't in this year's sessions, if you weren't dialling in, if you weren't privy to the conversations and exchanges, it feels important for me to state that these poems stand for so much more than you might be able to glean from a single PDF or printed publication.

So yes, we learned to love centos (there are a number here, including Bluey Little's *when their bones are picked, may a flower no more*), and some of us even learned to love paradelles (hats off to Rachel Lewis for making it look easy). We also learned to love our pond (with reference to an article from David Moldawer). We extended our love to the writer, teacher and maker Éireann Lorsung, who made her first appearance on the programme as a guest this year; and former co-tutor Rachel Long, who returned to support with feedback as seamlessly as if she'd never left. And we evolved. This year I was particularly happy to create space for the inaugural Legacy Lecture (the title may change, but thus far the alliterative effect has won out over the effort of coming up with anything more inventive)—a session led by a former BYP that I plan to continue as an annual fixture, this year delivered by Antosh Wojcik. We also welcomed another BYP baby to the fold (much love, Lauren B!), and a new member to the production team (nods to Blair Davis).

To end on that note of legacy: one of the key components of BYP's structure is the space we've made for people to take the programme three times; how a portion of each cohort is made up of people who've been through the programme in previous years. This was something I was keen to put in place from the very early days of the programme, and the sense of a body of poets that extends and is connected throughout the programme's history in very concrete ways is tangible and real. The ideal is that we hold space for each other, within and beyond the building. We constitute the ideal of the kinds of creative communities we want to see exist. In this, and many other ways, we author the world we want to be a part of. What's more powerful or transformative than that?

Jacob Sam-La Rose
Artistic Director and Lead Facilitator
Barbican Young Poets

Shyamli B

if revolution was a wall	**if revolution was a wall**
for now i seek a crack	for now i seek a crack
to squeeze	to squeeze
through	through
and out	and out
for now i seek the window	for now i seek the widow
i can smash	i am buried
with my mother's fists	in his garden
so now i wear a red cape	so now i wear a white coat
look for signs	look for signs
of her suffering	of my breathing
i grab her wrists	i dig for graves
scream at shards of glass	scream at blades of grass
there is still life left to live	*there is no life left to give*
for now i climb	for now he climbs
stairs on her shoulders	ladders on my laurels
take two steps to the door	takes two bullets to the floor
i whip mothers below me	he does not offer his shield
for not taking more	to those who need it more
now i meet her gaze	now i find my bones
with my guilt	in his casket
all the saving she didn't seek	all he stole as he left
if revolution was a wall	if revolution was a wall
i must be why it does not fall	he must be why it does not fall

for now i arrest my mother's husband
for crimes that taught me how to love

your God is not mine to meet
but your sins are mine to judge

i vomit
the peace she swallowed
to keep me alive

i point fingers at this hell
so what if this is home?

i almost forget
a woman is not a living thing
she is pet, in training
silly little girl

i almost forget
she must turn 18
when she is fifty

shrink
so i do not choke

i almost forget
i seek a crack
to squeeze
through
and out

but first i seek forgiveness
for the injustice

i was not simply a witness

for now i arrest my dead husband
for crimes that win the Nobel Prize

your God is not mine to meet
but my source is your disguise

i vomit
the war i swallowed
to keep him alive

i point rockets at his chest
so what if you were home?

i almost forget
a woman is not a killing rank
she is martyr, in waiting
suicide bomber

i almost forget
she must turn 18
when she is twelve

grow
so he does not choke

i almost forget
i seek a crack
to squeeze
through
and out

but first i seek reparations
for the injustice

i was simply a muse

Nomakhwezi Becker

A city, dreaming

Some nights
the tracks wail,
grinding on teary-eyed
metal, bloodshot rust
hangs on to morning joy
that never comes.
Howling out the dark
in tunnels that wind through
the belly of a city,
fireflies aglow
careening towards us.
Rows of cheap shoes
bought for temporary plans—
with scuffed foreheads,
once gleaming,
barely holding up
all these dreamers
still here years beyond
part-time imaginings,
preparations just
"for the time being".
Yet another late night
costumed for a story
none expected to star in.
But tickets are bought
for shrieking trains
to swallow us back
and forth between
shoeboxes and the wages
keeping our worlds

alive in them.
Some nights
the tracks wail,
hauling our hopes
into these entrails
of a city,
dreaming.

Summoned (The Wake)

There's flight in these hands
palms arched   then flat in landing

Lift off   soaring then landing again

                                        Ngiyeza[1]

In flight with them
I am raised by them
summoned to the grass mat
candle beside   holding vigil
smoke reaching after hands raised high

Palms fly
I   in them
soar   then land

                                        Ngiyeza

Summoned in the barrel of echoing thunderstorms
my cousin flies on   cowhide drum

Her palms arch   graze the heavens
catch our grandmother   soaring
land   again

                                        Ngiyeza

---

1   "I am coming" (isiZulu)

Sky broken open
these eyes shatter
and out falls a hurricane on troubled waters

Memories ripple   water drum
I with them
summoned back to shore

Ground beckons knees
when Mama breaks through the downpour
her voice whistles in my bones
ricochets in blood marrow drum

           Sabela uyabizwa![2]
             Ngiyeza

I answer
voice soars above hers
reaching for palms arched
that raised me soar   flatten
then land

          Gogo *Ngiyeza*

beating on stretched leather
skin of ancestor's dreams

Prying out old rhythms of sleepless nights
when   heart stuck in throat
asks pounding head

if hen dies and chicks scatter
who will gather us now

Fears hurtled against ribcage
their bodies my baseline

---

2 "Respond, you have been called" (isiZulu)

But here where hands fly
and voices collect debris mid-hurricane
Mama re-members us on grass mat
weaves song   womb of breath

Ancient birth midwived by prayers
holding the newborn
longing clasped tightly in each tiny hand

Fingers become wings that blow candle out
smoke billows our grandmother's calls
to beckon this infantile hope

There is flight in these hands

I am summoned

Gogo   Ngikhona[3]

Kneeling before all those I cannot walk without
even when Mama's voice and cousin's hands
are no longer near
and I tread far from home

Gogo   Sikhona[4]

---

3 "Grandmother, I am here" (isiZulu)
4 "Grandmother, we are here" (isiZulu)

Zad El Bacha

An Arab killed in Palestine

Even the dead will not be safe from the enemy if he is victorious. And this enemy has not ceased to be victorious. —Walter Benjamin, Theses on the Philosophy of History

Your corpse proves there was always
something rotten in you.
How easily your flesh starts
stinking, how you corrupt

yourself. Your corpse
proves your killer innocent.
As maggots crawl out of your eyes,
he points at you and says

does this look like a man to you?

Comrade, don't worry. I will answer
yes. And I love him,
and the blood pouring from his mouth
I will spit out of mine.

Geraint Ellis

G.F.A.R.

    I am G.F.A.R., I am
        marked as read
        and making sense,
  jostling for the
        half a Guinness, glass of house
          hang up on my second sister
     who is in my voicemail, I am
drafting a neighbourhood watch update on the terrible situation that is
        coursing through the terminal building
   jostling at the bar
  I am
marking emails
    halfway there
    watching neighbours
    glassing houses
        jostling at the bar I am
    a second sister
    sensing terror
    coursing through the
     jostling I am
  deleting all the voicemails I am
   planning for the spring
      I am
a halfway house and
    jostling and
no longer making sense I am
      a neighbourhood watch update I am
     dating out of terror and am
      muted by a voicemail and am
       halfway through an email and am

                    marking off the spring days and am
                        springing off the marks and I am
                            terrified of watching and
            am terminal at the bar and I am
coursing I am
        dying
I am
        G.F.A.F.R[1].

---

1   Goingforafuckingrun

Lava

We wade up to our nape lines,
shivering in the sink,
until our tiptoes tumble off the coal silt
and shingled-sand beneath—

sisters and I, sea swimming—

but even submerged
in a northern swell
we are aflame. A boreal forest-fire
is burning, carbon shrieking
in our bloodstream,
furious as molotovs
peeling back paint.

The exponential rate
of the growth
of our grief
means it is too large
and too recent
to be seen.

We are stood too close to this landscape.
The breadth of the sky is obscene.
The horizon is a lava rip, the thinnest wolf, shouting fire.

Nathalia Samhil Gonzalez Gutierrez

Habeas Corpus

There is a room behind every door, here,
there is a cheek, cold on the blue-tile floor.
There is a bed of black snakes trampled mid-slither by a head,
a stiff towel holding up a limp neck;
    abuelo had it embroidered with his name.
The mirror that saw los apagones erase my face
    slants towards the spiked waist.
There is a flashlight, expectant, on the sink
    but also a nationwide shortage of batteries.
There's a possibility the protruding ribs are my own,
                      the way bones are anybody's.
There is a rickety shower screen tickling the tips of abandoned feet and
a plastic tub sloshing half-empty with ration; it carries
a little tupperware inside, how, each day, I was baptised. Here,
there is only this miscarriage that keeps on miscarrying.
This room my children may never step foot in,
in a corner of a house a country once lived in.

oxytocin clumps at the cable input entrance (2019)

theres a vhs tape here ive been meaning not to see
labelled white
in a nordic language i cant read
something   mikkel   two thousand three
i hurl the plastic brick through
the window shatters
gives way to pink boys at sea
big brothers spin him by the pits
into the wailing vortex i once knew
im funnelled in the warm
whirl to thrash with her
reptile brain outlives intention
toward our beloved again
he giggles in the sun under brows
too   dark   for   his   eyes
those hazel eyes
mikkel said id curse our offspring
to see life without
the camera turns
hell always be his mothers smile
i stifle the devices nipple
under my thumb
imagine i am gouging out
his perfect pupil
from an olive.

Marianne Habeshaw

First time eating emu burgers at the bird sanctuary

My family observes
the emu cage.
Beaks so vengeful,
I realise
we're taking the piss.
Emu necks gulp
snooker balls.
They face us,
black—slits—amber.
My fear of being pecked
isn't selfish.
I question—any safety nets
that would stop it
beyond Mum's certain grief.
Saw the pink squares
in my Lunchables
differently.
Who pulls the weight
of its process?
Thought about Mum
busy in life's toy kitchen.
Saw in a manufacturer's video,
jumpsuits—pulling udders
under an icon of cheese.
Death lingered
in odd places.
Reading an article
on five-minute ways
to deal with mourning,
butter slurred

across my toast
became shit.
Took a bath
for some calm
after watching
a dinosaur documentary,
couldn't face
the silent history of water.
Birds were dinosaurs'
closest kin.
saw a Dromornis
in the tap's reflection.
pretty sure
it cursed me.
Left the bath
an emu,
eyes swollen
on my miracle neck.
Smelt burnt onions.
stubborn cooking
runs in my family.
Each waft,
a refusal
to turn the heat down.
Up our garden pathway,
oak mouths ajar
with blankness
given up to the sky.
I collapsed
on our lawn,
fenced in by gates.
An egg's fragile
hardness inside me.
Grass, spiking at my pelvis.
Pop!

How to: Modern Therapy

    1. En route, peel silver birch to warm up to epiphany
until a lime strip slaps your face.
    2. Your self-diagnosis frees your therapist
from assumption you'll be restrained.
    3. Confess your problem:
milk one trauma so hard the udder turns to ash. If she looks confused,
it might be a mixed metaphor; improve.
    4. Say you're a micro-sculptor,
working in the off-beats of your heart rate. No pleasure until the end.
    5. If she reaches for a leaflet, it's too intense.
    6. Say you're fine, except for the migraine
from skipping in a rubble car park/ chopping peppers in your kitchen
so rough they stay whole.
    7. Predictably, she'll say separating night and day
is healthy. Everyone knows time's true shape is a fracture.
    8. Admit regrets.
Sometimes, you stroke a photograph like a baby's head.
It feels one-sided.
    9. She'll ask where you are mentally at this moment,
where memories are ghostlike before gripping sleep.
    10 Tell her you're removing your bra at a couples' retreat
        (a sad metal shack)—
an ex watches your earrings burst into flame
but won't unhook them with unbrushed teeth.

Oli Isaac

vultures will only care about me when i'm dead, or dying, or sick

i cough and beg to be noticed   pretend to choke on my water   no-one turns around
we sit on the edge of the landfill   white-tipped wings swoop down mistake prawn crisp
packets for fish heads   our out-of-sights our out-of-minds exposed to a divine sun

a beak tears into a black plastic bag   unnecessarily graceful shadows mock chiaroscuro
a kid shouts *buitres!* as he cycles past   they are common as pigeons here   you shout
basureros back   binmen   and i wonder what it's like to rely on the dead

to recycle and reuse and reduce the dead whether it's less messy this way or if they wished to
feel a warmth just once   a forager   cursed to be a scavenger mistaken as a predator

i wonder how they can tell   heat vision or   i close my eyes for a minute play dead no-one
takes the bait and you say *whatever they don't eat was never alive in the first place*   and i
take it to mean much more than you meant it to mean

i bet they can taste the long, good lives.   you tell me to stop romanticising at the rubbish dump *and that maybe they can see the becoming*   like how that boy on our street suddenly became less instead of more   and the fire last night was until it wasn't   and we will become barely and sorry for not replying   and the flowers become tired but only for a season   and the sweat at your temples   and the redness of your hands against mine and the fingernails of your whole being clinging onto this   stupid   moment before it ripens into something worth scavenging

why can't i say it straight?

i want to write you love poems
but i write   away   and   away
and then toward but in the margins and between the lines and repeat
i am getting lost in efforts to subvert google docs need to capitalise every new line

we sit on the side of a mountain huddled under a bent tree shaped by years and years and
years of wind   the slowness of it all slides down my throat and sits there in silence

you slice a banana with a knife and stir the porridge
i notice you could ruin my life and that maybe i want you
to wipe away language   and pasts i thought i could fix
strip for parts the theseus ship of my body
that always took on water when it lingered too long at port
leave nothing to trip up on leave me light

blast me with x-ray radiation so i can check there is nothing hiding behind my collarbone
nothing beyond the visible electromagnetic spectrum
from the times i refused to let go
       left to soak overnight
           i can compare and contrast for twelve points

i am bloated with so many past lives
like that simpson episode when homer becomes the sanitation commissioner and buries all the
waste under springfield and it explodes through lecterns and mailboxes and golf courses
an exorcist peels it back   the echo feels like a bass   they all end up sounding the same

sorry
i was told to write it slant
and my feet lost grip in the dunes
and there was no path out of it

sorry
what i mean to say is
found somewhere in between
the oxalis propagating on my desk
and the sound of keys clicking in the lock of our door

Noah Jacob

if the black holes come for us

I'd say, Mum.

They're in the garden. Wrestling.

Mum, they're sweaty. Heaving. Slipping
through each other's binaries. Spaghettifying apart.
Trying to make enough spacetime.

But they're dirty.

I'd say, Mum, our house is falling apart.
They've cut our benefits again.

*I want to do something but I feel too old, too over-
encumbered with shadows to care.*

I'd say, So another sun died last week and I closed my eyes to it. Just needed a nap.
I'd —

so if the black holes come for us nuclear shadows would vestigialise the shape of you
after the state explodes at you tonight the detonation would be swallowed I would
hold on to you for dear life

say it all.
Below working class is cosmic redundancy.

photon and antiphoton would collide and we'd still be cold this winter

And somehow
with all this entropy,
I'd say *the cosmic dust settled perfectly.*

But it's okay Mum, you'll be anointed with their oils.
We'll stink of the Big Bang.
At our funerals they'll wrestle instead of dance.

The jazz swing of the end of things.

salmon run

thank god I've never seen
a salmon pray.
bent rigid towards the Sun,
operculum open and blubbering.

they are born into freshwater,
come of age in the ocean
and swim back again to lay eggs.
anadromous
they run anadromous,
parabolic swing back into
miles of amniotic salt and

somewhere, along the string,
the bears catch them,
give life for life,
crush smokened soft bodies until
the spill of roe from the wound and
still—
they struggle to prostrate
to the Sun. instead, are
discipled into molar pews.
the sufi sway of the willows
gives grace to a good hunt.

and thank god for their eyes,
a tide of exoskeleton
curved in two dimensions,
magnetite pulled fishheaded
into

sometimes, the programming glitches.
a body that doesn't
know its enemy.

a burning,
down the knots
in both legs.
bedbound, fleshbound,
as dead and alive
as the
salmon.

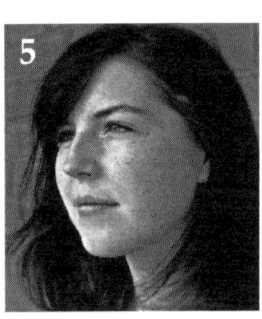
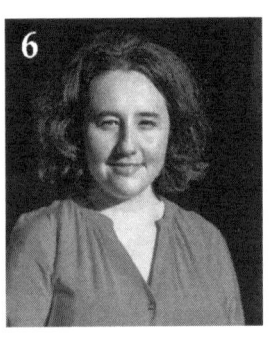

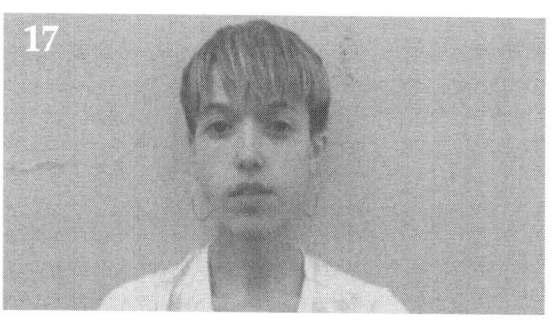

Kerrica Kendall

Morsel in a history

eyes up
hmm
.......this taste......so familiar.......
& on the tip of my ensemble tastebuds + I
am unfamiliar in words
so if I were to spell you, right now "c o n f u s e"

I play with the foods in my barn mouth, I know I know you,
this sensation finding me again........
Hi   how long has it been

CAVERNOUS,,, BEAMS ,,,,,, YOUR TEMPLE,,,,,,I'M COMMITTED
grinding rice into wet over and over
my tongue
hitting my cheeks   rotating   binding   fibres selecting their toothstay's

I like it here, they say

even my lungs remember you and you are a welcomed flavour
           oh we've met before

           you don't seem to meet my gaze
     that I crush for   equals

so I'm pulsing fibres   gathering strays   slipping   to find your alphabet
I wish I could reject my saliva for a moment whether it'll cost me ours, I want your name
     but your language jumbling   since when were you running ahead?
                                      now you're quieting before me
                                  in half many

                    am I possessive
                     made in charge of this gulp

I'm sorry for my unfamiliarity   in   I   doesn't begin in here

let me hear you? out of my skull?   do you   will you accept me?

                this tongue?

                        again?

                                I lean in for another bite

                                        and another

                                                and another

Palatable
after Broken & Beirut by Sahueir Hammad

At the table,
a beheaded strawberry brought to eyeline to discern its redness
is still lit, dimming, without its stem
and the scene is loaded with, say, blueberries, chocolate,
would you like a cup of tea? how nice is unfiltered tea—to choose your
experience of weather

/ Would you like some diced potato?
made thirsty, small potato cubes collapsing at the corners?
Sir, we have no fuel to cook them
could you wait until they distintegrate without a cover, would you like to
watch as it happens
your eyes seem ready enough, your dancing for fruit salads is—
a catastrophe dressed this bowl, tossing white liquids, are they your fruits,
is this your harvest?

dangerous fruits, dangerous fruits, chocolate, and honey,
gauzed in made-to-last packs,
finger nimble sachets of ketchup waved in a forefinger and
memory of a blueberry,
grapes and cake in agreement and cream as
airy as bone you like to crunch is that

stains
and mug rims—tea stains—
the tea stains in tea water—all your fabrics—
all your—knife perpendicular even when it's empty
I pray you run out of energy you dry your mouth forensic—

the kitchen has soaked in your efforts, the kitchen—we were all born as cream cake—why are you trying to gas it a non definition—somehow you're axing your play on a sliced-deep board somehow we can all taste it no we know how and we're not in your kitchen is it—it is saved under my tummy (by all) we swallowed its memory we swallow the overflowing unsavoury, savour its ugly, memory, this little strawberry in a factory.

Rachel Lewis

Honestly

What if they never take the Christmas lights down?
what if the red white blue scrolling
of the barbershop neon light gets stuck?
what if the sun only ever rises, and what if
every wrinkle in the pavement finds a speaking voice,
what if the way I was made wasn't made for this?
what if I dug deep and pulled the topsoil over myself
like a blanket, with cigarette butts for crumbs
and Victorian sewer drains for company? what if
every single bus is going to your house
and what if hours sour under my tongue,
what if I lose my breath and never catch it,
what if today was the last day I could have saved myself
and I didn't even know and I did nothing about it
as the sky lilacs into heat death darkness
and what if I didn't even warn you,
what if fear so electric that it will separate
skin from sinew is coming for me
like tea stains sinking into teeth,
what then, darling, what then?

Diamond paradelle

A diamond ring is waiting in the drawer.
A DIAMOND RING is waiting in the drawer
and nobody believes it should be mine.
And nobody believes! It should be mine,
the ring believes nobody and is waiting
in a diamond drawer. It should be mine.

When the ring came in the post for him, I stole it.
When the ring came in the post for him I stole it
then I laughed and gave it back to him.
Then I laughed. And gave it back to him,
then the post laughed, stole it back for him,
and when I came to him, I gave it in, the ring.

On bonfire night he made the ring a joke.
On bonfire night he made the ring a joke—
the lawyer asked me to explain my reasons.
The lawyer asked me to explain. My reasons
on a night bonfire, my joke reasons,
he asked / made me explain the ring to the lawyer.

The lawyer laughed and stole the ring and reasons.
He made me explain the ring should be mine.
Then I came back to him, gave it when asked.
I joke it is in the post for him to—
Nobody believes it! My ring on a bonfire.
A night diamond, waiting in the drawer.

Bluey Little

Archimedes' Principle

"you don't look back along time but down through it, like water. sometimes this comes to the surface, sometimes that, sometimes nothing. nothing goes away."
— *Elaine Risley, Cat's Eye (Margaret Atwood)*

the theory goes that if you draw a bowhead whale
to the surface of the arctic, there is an absence, and
                the absence of a whale is water

and if water always seeks
itself, temperance upright,
ever boundless & refilling
                        do the other whales notice? do they

nudge its freshness with suspicion,
as a hermit to December?

when they glide through its current,
does the absence still sing?

when their bones are picked, may a flower no more

open their wounds for me, wide as an english west moon. each day, I keep out the god so that I shall not break. always the same, this frenzy, like riding alone on the subway in the time allotted for lovers.

as the small hours open, a flower looks toward me. I keep out the god doubtfully.

after Anne Sexton, Larry Levis, Dylan Thomas, Simone Muench, Ingeborg Bachmann, Octavio Paz, Henri Michaux, Agnes Nemes Nagy, Joyce Mansour, William Burroughs, Meret Oppenheim, Mary Low, Adrienne Rich, & Carl Sandburg

Katie O'Pray

In my slice of city

I haven't spoken aloud all day. I have ventured 60 miles
to now, where I'm among some well-thought-out
benches, a homogenous brickwork pavement. Blossom
flocking the trees; coveted, ripe & bulbous, touching hues
with the sky. A creek is audible, uninterested in the rising
value of its banks. Nobody seems to mind me, in my slice
of city, tucked behind the church's back. The ruins of a wall
imply a history worth preserving. I wonder about this density
of people, the ancient masonry, surrounding windows, little boxed
-up lives. Laundry & lamps & mutual overlookedness. I wonder
about the mother lugging groceries past me, teaching her daughter
beauty. To gather petals please, no feathers, no leaves. Scattered
gardens are wriggling with workers & groups laughing in thin
jackets, sucking at the last dregs of dusk. Its peachy
settle. There's a couple taking photos with long
technical lenses. Lily pads. Reflections. My face
opened up toward the skyscrapers, unoccupied
by its usual thoughts. I am not alone. I am not alone
in my appreciation of this moment, these brief fruits
of a meagre winter. There's an ephemeral mood about,
like many heads tuning into the same happy thought.
The streetlamp begins to nag. Signs of life moving
from the ground to the birdsong, into the vast flight
paths. Light blooming up the ribs of the tower blocks.

Becoming Auntie

When you were born, I was feeble, in the winter of myself. I took to walking
the frost for hours, with your pram to hold me up, singing aloud. My chest had
too many unhealthy hollows, the opposite of soothing, but I held you anyway. It felt
strange, wanting thicker arms. Mine were pathetic, once buckled & I watched you
bounce off the carpet. Said *I'm sorry I'm sorry I'm so sorry* to your mum. You
couldn't understand apologies so I could only show you, become safer, get big
& strong. You could feel my lap widening, more room, my hands less cold
when I stroked your head. I softened everywhere. I followed your lead
onto solid foods – sliced bananas & Wotsits, things that are easy to chew.
I couldn't be sure what you were taking in so I was always modelling
kind hands in case. Gentle words, even as you slept. When you held out
a chocolate button, I'd say *Ta*. Swallow, grin, rub my tummy. It taught us
both a lesson – what we were willing to give up, out of love. Eating
got easier once you'd grown into sandwiches, after you'd first managed
my name, bending it through your smile, its syllables catching on
your two teeth. I loved being that sound. It was summer then & our nurses
were pleased with how we were growing. We were no longer
waking in the night, crying out to be fed.

Beth Phillips

pit bonk wench

we are built of rubber & steel
sat in hot iron
until our puddlers burn.
like a great oak set alight
until we are nothing but bones.

& it's october but still hotter than july
& the fury us three feel is enough
to turn bystanders to tears.

we are bonded through cities,
pull at handbrakes
last minute,
face first to the bridges
but never the water.
& we wonder whether next year
will be different,
move into new homes,
collect trinkets left on street corners.

& sometimes the months until we meet
feel still, so we work & thirst & struggle
with silence until we speak again,
thirty feet underground.

when my mother became an egg

I carried her to the sea. we watched lifeboats sink
while she whispered, *we're not so different*
that when I become an egg, I would have to find some other spot
to be buried in   it's inevitable   time walks still
on the waterfront. but for a moment I thought I heard her
in another drink, our faces merging, seeing misery in portrait mode.

and I watched it happen over time, the way her body curled
and flinched with sudden noise. how she started to shrink
when the tablets started working and her voice became flat.
and I was a child. how selfish of me, waiting at the school gates
when she was watching
moonlight, six foot deep in oncology.

and when we lay upon the beach, she cracked, muted resentment
kept in a square mile radius. it's simple, I grieve for something
that isn't mine, the time we didn't get to spend together.
does the pain pass or do we forget how it felt?
will I remember what she was like before I collected the shell
that rattled when it moved?

Jess Rahman-González

I told u hell is emotional intimacy & u still kissed me (a cento)

Need something awful done to my body
Chemist said it would be alright
Never been the same since
Didn't mince my words   said
Heaven's a wound I pass through
To the grief-wracked city
Nerves are bad tonight
Yes   bad
Made my house my gallows
Stay with me
I will spare you my body
Just speak to me
He asks how many men
I've fucked this month
Not loved
And I fell
As all bodies fall
For dead

Sources: [Dante Alighieri, T.S. Eliot, Sam Sax]

Amani Saeed

In flagrante

I revelled in another's arms last night,
came apart under his touch.
His kisses trailed my skin like kites.

I pressed into his hands, soft clutch,
and did my best to disappear.
I didn't think of you that much.

His lashes were long, eyes twin deer,
mouth warm and soft as flame.
He traced my spine. Drew me near.

Though it could not be the same,
I still hoped—then quit the fight.
Never again will you call my name.

So I took our tenderness, held it to the light
and killed it, love.
I revelled in another's arms last night.

When I come back
a cento for Palestine

I can't say who I am
unless you agree I'm real.
Whenever I sit for a while, my elbow digging
into my thigh, my head in my hands,
I am a meditative stranger
massaging his stranger's thigh.
I call to things; I'll sing
in the vernacular of a young basil stem.
Nothing brings me back from my faraway.
Was the road always like this, a messenger
calling? I, with two wings
that happened suddenly,
went out looking for my house– if you're not
home, where are you?–
my house, strong from years of fantasy,
that glimmers
for the far upon the far.
Who am I, without exile?
We are now loosened
from the gravity of identity's land—
everything speaks its own language.
I am real, and I can't say who I am. I am he
who was one day me.
Whatever night grew, a pact of horrors,
a pact of marvels, I'd have to carry him
between my teeth.
I devoured what others thought
I was nourishing, had no time
to stop and kiss your hand, to speak

of my need for love. It doesn't matter.
Once we're flames, you won't be able to tell
one of us from the other; when we die, we give
our names back.

Amna Muhammad Abu Safat, Mahmoud Darwish, Zakaria Mohammed, Mourid Barghouti, Maya Abu Al-Hayyat, Amiri Baraka, Shira Erlichman.

Lucas Sheridan

Plucked
After Yalie Saweda Kamara

There's bird call from two teenage boys in the parking lot.
They creep closer, gull-footed
and knock-kneed, across white marked lines.

Their wings blister up like blooms
of mould and they are magnificently lost,
unable to home

in on anything but this. They know touching
is emptying their own nests
but stretch their full spans, feathers extending

how fingers cannot. Up there—or maybe I mean here—the air
is truly on their faces for the first time in years. It stings like
sherbet sweets and laughter. It's like the earth

no longer needs an axis. They are
gliding, whooping, loop-the-looping.
Pecking, beckoning, becoming.

They call again
far beyond the white lines and narrow streets
where they get driven home in separate cars.

They call again
and the sound flows
over the backs of new found flocks.

They call again, birds now, and think
how tarmac will never feel the same beneath their feet.

Maeve Slattery

Massage

It's Sunday, and I wake to gold
streaming in through
the window, over
our faces.

I show you,
shaping my hands
as goggles to your wide,
loving eyes. You smile.

I dot-to-dot down
the freckles on
your arms,
imagining
them roaring
in spring. Your body
is textured with tides, ebbing
in and out. Reasonless now.
I follow rivers with you.

Take tension on a
voyage.

Whatever
your water form,
however you are named.

In a Moment of Future Brightness
After 'All the Women Caught in Flaring Light' by Minnie Bruce Pratt

There I am, washing up mugs to make tea whilst my Butch nestles behind me.
She wraps her arms around my waist, gently touching my bump belly.
Or the window testifies to her soapy hands, my sweetpea arms enveloping.

I'm unsure yet if there's a baby inside her, or me, or whether we've just finished
an abundant meal. We're divinely creative anyway.

My Butch clicks the kettle before the steam gets too loud and we prepare our
stored herbs as teas: mint, rosemary, lemon balm, sage. Neither of us applies
pressure, allowing the leaves to take their time.

On the table is a vase of flowers, birthed together from seed: calendula,
borage, lavender, gypsophila.

In the next room, our chosen family, or some of them, laugh and chat busily
as birds, uninterrupted by our absence.

My Butch rests her head on my chest as I hold her close, stroking the moss
of her neck. We sway together, rooted.

Beneath us, generations of dykes dance, mycorrhizal network to us saplings,
our sweetness in memory of theirs. We feed their ruptured families; they
scavenge the ruins of history for mineral nutrients.

Minnie said, *Things have been done to us that can never be undone.*

Yet here we are, miraculous. Might just burst and become a blur, hoping:

we can have children, if we choose them.
Our lives will have softness, if we pay attention.
A river of love flows forever, if we make it so.

Ishita Uppadhayay

English Education

How many convent schools in India?
Too many Loretos, made by those missionaries.
A mission is a quest, implying a goal.
In a photo, I see my mum at a school race.
Year 5, her smile, track lines on mud,
three Irish nuns, seated, white
like their plastic chairs.

The best school in Lucknow, Uttar Pradesh?
Loreto Convent, my grandma said, so there Richa went,
reciting *Give us our daily bread*,
hallowed be thy name,
our Father in Heaven,
lead us not into temptation,
do lead her safely home
to finish schoolwork in a living room
adorned with Radha, Krishna, Shiva and the lot.

Sister Mary, Sister Nora, Sister Anna
forbade Hindi, said, *Speak it at home*.
Instructed discipline on knuckles,
extra English lessons after school.

Cultural imperialism: Indians taught in English.
Now I speak a mongrel mix.
My granddad speaks only *shuddh* Hindi.
I spot a rainbow, he quotes Wordsworth—
the English that he knows.
To speak "purely" in my native language,
my mother's tongue,
is to keep English words out.

Machine

Commuting home reading emails cos they pre-load. When I was little, I'd scan labels on shampoo when on the toilet. I'd succumb to brain rot if I had WiFi on the Tube. I read the weekly newsletter of a non-partisan-crowdfunded-democratic-digital-only media outlet. The author is 30, writes of experiencing two no-fault evictions in nine years of renting in London, does a strong analysis: these are the bills that failed. These are the groups that lobbied. These are the ones who profit. Little council housing, many holiday rentals. Are economies ever doomed? Economies should only grow, scale, rise from local to global. Are nations ever doomed? My nation-state isn't a state until it competes. My state is also on a "world stage". We are measured against the yardsticks of others. How is our economic performance? Are we dancing? The faces of England's commuters betray apathy. There are mechanics involved, economies shift, accelerate. Growth is lifeless. A line "moves" on a graph but it is still. If the rentals create wealth, so be it. If the wealth is concentrated, so be it. We favour numbered largesse; we need increase. A machine was only ever a tool to extract more from the same. The soot-filled quality of the air doesn't go away when you leave the Underground.

Vera K Yuen

Self-Portrait as Lampshade

When Dad straightens his spine,
    it bears weight without a creak,
heaped with dishes.

Beyond the shuttered door,
    no one knows I'm a standing lamp on guard
sweating through the crimped fabric shade

uncloaking the shadows.

My words contain the bite of tungsten
    coiled within my glass bulb throat.
I am demure, capable of

switching moods with a flick of Mum's conductor wrist.
    Better to confuse the moth-mouthed neighbors
than to singe their wings.

Tragedy swims behind our closed eyelids.
    Our hands orbit the dinner table:
weapons we have to carve up arguments like

Christmas roast. We pull at the tendons
    and wait for the unraveling.
As if conjured,

orchids animate out of Mum's hands
    and curl towards mine,
their stems bowed in reverence.

Love is the violent bruise
    blooming over my knuckles,
the night scraped raw.

Biographies

Shyamli B[7]
Shyamli is a writer based in London. In the day (and night!) she works in investment banking at Goldman Sachs, and recently began writing as a way to make sense of her incongruence with the world around her. Prior to finance, Shyamli worked across the public, private and non-profit sector in Asia, Europe and the US: writing at The Economist, studying Southeast Asian economies, and leading various activism efforts across politics, public health, and social work. She studied at Harvard Business School and the University of Oxford, and has been writing over the last few years to rediscover her authenticity, identity and creativity after many years on a path where she lost sight of it. She currently posts her writing on Substack, TikTok and Instagram under the pseudonym *badgersett*.

Nomakhwezi Becker[3]
Nomakhwezi Becker is a South African-German interdisciplinary artist creating through the written word, theatre, storytelling and poetry performance. Her practice explores the call and response of collaborative distant intimacy when finding, reclaiming and creating home in the in-between spaces as a woman raised by multiple homes, heritages and languages. Through her work she hopes to create worlds that hold space for dialogue around exploring our 'in-betweenity' as citizens of the world.

Zad El Bacha[13]
Zad is a writer and community organiser from London. They were one of the winners of the 2019 Spread the Word London Writers Awards, and have written on migration, feminism and colonialism for VICE, Red Pepper, The Vision and AZ-magazine. They have written theatre shows preserving oral family histories of war for the Camden People's Theatre and the North Wall. They were commissioned by Poet in the City and their poetry was published in Bad Betty Press' *Field Notes on Survival* and *the other side of hope*. They are currently writing their first novel, an extract from which won the Peggy Chapman-Andrews First Novel Award 2022. They hope to see the end of capitalism in their lifetime.

Geraint Ellis[12]
Geraint Ellis is a Barbican Young Poet and former Scottish National Slam Poetry Finalist. He has been shortlisted for the Aesthetica Creative Writing Prize, Bridport Prize, Aurora Prize and Hexham Poetry Competition, and twice long-listed for the National Poetry Competition. His work is published by *flipped eye publishing*, *Broken Sleep Books*, *Abridged* and more. He has written extensively for BBC Radio Comedy.

Marianne Habeshaw[1]
Marianne is a queer poet from Peterborough, currently residing in North London. She is the founder/producer of Thoughtcast Collective, which organises multidisciplinary art shows at St. Margaret's House. Her work has been highly commended for the Outspoken Page Poetry Prize, and she has been longlisted for the same prize twice. She has been published by LADA, Enthusiastic Press, and long-listed for Butcher's Dog. Additionally, she has upcoming anthology publications with Flipped Eye and Off The Chest Anthology. Her work explores themes such as the movements/refusals of time and memory through the systems and cycles of capitalism, grounded in the body and desire. Her poetry applies the logic of cartoon-time and chaos.

Oli Isaac[14]
Oli Isaac is a London-based playwright and poet, who likes to write tender poems about their tender thoughts. They are interested in how language can fail us, and how experiments in poetry and multimedia can attempt to cross that gap. Oli is a recipient of Audible Theatre's Emerging Playwrights Fund and most recently the winner of the 2024 Verve Poetry Festival Competition.

Noah Jacob[10]
Noah Jacob is an Arab-British poet, performer and critic based in London. Her writing often explores boundaries between human and unhuman, interrogating the poetry within biology, automaton and nature, particularly the ocean.
She is an alum of the Roundhouse Poetry Collective 2021/22, having placed second in the Roundhouse Poetry Slam 2021. She is an editor and co-writes a column on diaspora poetry for Zindabad Zine. She is also an alum of Apples and Snakes 'The Writing Room' and T.S. Eliot Prize Young Critics. Her work has been featured by the National Poetry Library, Shubbak, Camden Inspire and Peckham Festivals, and published in *orangepeel*, *Hecate*, and *Kalopsia* mags.

Noah is currently working on a poetry-music E.P., exploring themes of heritage and intergenerational relationships, nature and mythology and religion. In Summer 2024, she will be featured at *The Last Word* Festival and *05Fest: Redacted*.

Kerrica Kendall[2]
Kerrica Kendall is an actor, writer, and aspiring director.

Rachel Lewis[6]
Rachel Lewis is a poet and creative facilitator interested in hidden pain, everyday joy and love beyond romance. Her first pamphlet, 'Three degrees of separation', was published by Wordsmith HQ after winning the Wordsmith Prize. Individual poems have been published by bath magg, Under the Radar, Ink, Sweat and Tears, and the Poetry Society, among others. She is a recipient of the 2022 Jewish Book Week Emerging Writers Award and co-founder of Disabled Joy: the Writing Happiness Project. She can be found at @rachel_lewis_poet on Instagram and twitter.

Bluey Little[5]
Bluey (she/they) is a hot mess of air signs who likes making plays & poems. A self-described Weegie/Loiner mongrel, they are currently based in North London.
Areas they are often drawn to include queerness, nature, & the liminal. Since developing long covid in the summer of 2022, their work has also been dialogue with (or running from) their condition. Mostly, they just like rubbing words together and seeing what kindles.
Barbican Young Poets marks the first work Bluey has produced since diagnosis. You can find more of them & their work at https://blueylittle.carrd.co.

Katie O'Pray[8]
Katie O'Pray is a creative facilitator, based in Bedford. They have been the winner of the ruth weiss Foundation's Emerging Poet's Prize and the Oxford Brookes International Poetry Competition. Their work has also earned recognition in the National Poetry Competition, the Manchester Writing Competition and the Magma Poetry Competition, among others. Their 'devastating' debut collection 'APRICOT' was published by Out-Spoken Press in 2022.

Beth Phillips[19]
Beth Phillips is a Birmingham based poet focused on the confessional form. A graduate of BA (Hons) in Creative Writing, and MA Arts Management, her work explores community, family and grief. She has previously founded a multidisciplinary magazine, showcasing the voices of emerging artists.

Jess Rahman-González[17]
Jess Rahman-González (they/them) is a writer and performer working across poetry, theatre, and live art. Their work currently focuses on their experiences of being on inpatient eating disorder wards.

Previously, Jess has been a Barbican Open Labs artist and Starting Blocks resident artist at Camden People's Theatre. They have also been part of Roundhouse Poetry Collective, Soho Theatre's Writers' Lab and Royal Court's playwriting group.

Amani Saeed[18]
Amani Saeed is an international writer who treads the line between roots and routes. She writes poetry, blog posts, films, and whatever else is needed to get the point across. Amani is the curator and host of of the interdisciplinary sell-out night the hen-nah party, designed by and for queer South Asians. Her poetry collection, Split, was published with Burning Eye Books. Amani is the co-writer for Queer Parivaar, which premiered at the BFI Flare 2022 and won Best in British at the Iris Prize 2022.

Nathalia Samhil Gonzalez Gutierrez[11]
Nathalia Samhil Gonzalez Gutierrez is a Venezuelan, London-based poet and feminist community organiser; raised across four continents, her writing explores displacement, collective grief, and its role in socio political change. She's a co-founder of Tangled Tongues / Lenguas Enredadas - a Spanglish writing group whose eponymous zine is currently in the National Poetry Library's collection. She is also the Alastair Mcbain Scholar for International Human Rights Law at Oxford University, where she has been researching transitional justice and economic violence. She'll be spending the next few months working with civil society organisations in Venezuela and Colombia.

Lucas Sheridan[4]
Lucas Sheridan is a queer student and poet based whose writing deals with gender, queerness, the natural world, and health. He is a Nine Arches Press Dynamo Mentee, Barbican Young Poet, and Unislam

2023 winner. His poetry has been published in Queerlings, Eponym, and Inkwell and won a Young Poets' Network Challenge. You can find them in gardens on cold mornings with a cup of tea, at your local open mic night, or in kitchens at parties telling their friends to join a union.

Maeve Slattery[15]

Maeve is a Femme dyke from South London with a love for poetic balm-making. She is a Barbican Young Poet alum, with two poems in flipped eye's 2022 anthology: 'Articulations for Keeping the Light In'. She was longlisted for Culture Recordings' New Voice in Poetry Prize 2020. Maeve collects seeds, grows flowers and makes her own skincare products from infused oils. She has run creative workshops for young people in and leaving the care system across London and is a community organiser for The Equality Trust. You can find her on Instagram: @maeve_slattery_

Ishita Uppadhayay[16]

Ishita Uppadhayay is a writer and policy professional from India based in London. Their poetry has been featured in Phi Mag, the87pres, and STRAND Mag. They can be found at @ishitaupp.

Vera K Yuen[9]

Vera K Yuen is a poet and writer born and raised in Hong Kong. Her work is featured or forthcoming on PN Review, The Lumiere Review and elsewhere. Previously, she was the winner of the Charles Causley International Poetry Competition 2022 and was highly commended in the Disabled Poets Prize 2024. She is a current Barbican Young Poet and a keen mental health advocate. Every long-lived experience is made up of a series of discrete moments. Steps along the path from wherever the history began to wherever we've arrived at, now.

Also from Barbican Young Poets

Articulations for Keeping the Light In (2022)
To Be Languaged Thus (2023)